Land
The Geography of Salvation

LEADER'S GUIDE

Stephen J. Binz

LITTLE ROCK SCRIPTURE STUDY

*A ministry of the Diocese of Little Rock
in partnership with Liturgical Press*

CONTENTS

The Program Defined   5

Elements of the Program   5
    Prayer Services   5
    Taped Lectures   6
    Small-Group Discussions   6
    Personal Study   7

Program Materials   8

Program Schedule   9
    Schedule for Four Weekly Sessions   10
    Schedule for Eight Weekly Sessions   11

Coordinator Responsibilities   13

Support Team   13

Small-Group Facilitators   15

Techniques for the Small-Group Facilitator   15

Facilities and Equipment   17

Preparations   18

Timeline for Preparation   21

Directions for the First Session   22

Use and Care of Video Tapes   23

Answer Guide   24

The Program Defined

Lands of the Bible encourages participants to study the connections between the biblical text and biblical geography. It provides an overview of the places of the Bible where God's presence has become manifest to the people of God throughout the biblical periods. It also helps participants to relate some of the biblical places and landscapes to the places and experiences of their own lives. The places of our salvation speak their own message just as the biblical text speaks its message.

This program is for anyone who wishes to go on a visual and imaginative pilgrimage through the lands that are now called holy. Whether or not you will physically travel to these lands, the holy places provide learning and inspiration for the spiritual life. This course will enrich your understanding of the Bible and will help you visualize the places mentioned in the biblical texts.

The program takes an experiential approach to learning consisting of prayer, home study, group discussion, and video lectures. It is designed to be used with a group of people who will provide encouragement, support, and shared insight for one another. Through watching, listening, reflecting, praying, and conversing, participants will come to a fuller understanding of the living Word of God.

The program may be used in a number of different settings. It works well for adult religious education programs or for Scripture study groups. It may also be used in homes, in small faith communities, Sunday school, and neighborhood groups.

Elements of the Program

PRAYER SERVICES

Each weekly session begins with a prayer service. The service is designed to encourage the group to reflect on some aspect of the biblical lands to be studied in the lesson to follow. The prayer helps the group to open their minds and hearts and to focus on the Scriptures.

The content of the prayer services is provided in the Participant's Book. The leaders may want to add additional elements such as songs, an enthroned Bible, candles, and seasonal or thematic accents for the environment.

TAPED LECTURES

The informational content of this program is provided through eight lectures on video tape. These lectures are outlined in the Participant's Book so that participants are able to follow along and add personal notes if they wish.

The first lecture will survey the places of the Bible as they have been experienced by pilgrims through the ages. Connections will be made between the journeys of our biblical ancestors and our own experiences as a pilgrim people today.

The following lectures look at the biblical geography of the desert, the waters, and the mountains. Lectures 2, 3, and 4 explore the places within this biblical topography and the significance of these places for our own journey in the wilderness, through the waters, and up the mountains.

Lecture 5 describes the towns and places associated with the conception, infancy, and childhood of Jesus. Lecture 6 describes the region of Galilee, the primary place for the teaching and healing ministry of Jesus and his disciples.

The seventh lecture looks at the rich history of Jerusalem, from its conquest by David and the age of the Temple to the passion, death, and resurrection of Jesus. The last lecture shows the results of Jesus' final commission—to spread the good news to the ends of the earth. It discusses the places of Paul's travels as well as the places of John's writings.

SMALL-GROUP DISCUSSIONS

Each weekly session includes group discussion based on questions from the Participant's Book. The first session contains questions that can be discussed and researched quickly in the group. Subsequent discussions are based on the written responses to the personal study questions prepared in advance by each member of the group.

The questions for group discussion need not be limited to the questions in the Participant's Book. Another question that would be appropriate to ask in each discussion is this: "What were the main insights you received from the lecture you just watched?"

The discussion allows participants to grow in their understanding as they share insights with others in the group. They will begin to build a supportive community that encourages one another to continue daily reflection on the Scriptures.

The facilitator of each group may use the Answer Guide found toward the end of this book. The Answer Guide is to be used only during the facilitator's preparation time and not during the actual group discussion. The Answer Guide insures that the facilitators have a good understanding of each question so that they can guide the discussion more effectively.

PERSONAL STUDY

Between each session participants study the Bible at home. The only resources necessary are a modern translation of the Bible and the Participant's Book. The Participant's Book contains questions for study and reflection. Space is provided for writing responses to each.

The personal study continues to explore the information given in the weekly lectures. Some questions deepen the participants' understanding of what was learned; others anticipate the material to be learned in the next lecture. Many questions synthesize the elements learned from the program and encourage a personal application of the Scriptures to contemporary life.

These questions and written responses form the basis of the weekly discussion.

Program Materials

- **The Bible**

    Participants will each need a Bible. Any good, recent translation is fine.

- **Participant's Book**

    One book is needed for each participant. This contains prayer services, outlines for each lecture, and questions for personal study.

- **Leader's Guide**

    One guide is needed for each facilitator and program leader.

- **Video Lectures**

    Two video tapes contain eight lectures, providing the content for this program.

- **Video Player and Monitor**

Program Schedule

This program may be adapted to the time and needs of the group. Here are a few options:

A four-week program lasting an hour and a half each week:

Welcome and prayer service *(10 minutes)*
A taped lecture *(25 minutes)*
Small-group discussion *(30 minutes)*
A taped lecture *(25 minutes)*

A four-week program lasting two hours each week:

Welcome and prayer service *(10 minutes)*
A taped lecture *(25 minutes)*
Small-group discussion *(35 minutes)*
Break *(15 minutes)*
A taped lecture *(25 minutes)*
Prayer service *(10 minutes)*

An eight-week program lasting 55 minutes each week:

Welcome and prayer service *(10 minutes)*
A taped lecture *(25 minutes)*
Small-group discussion *(20 minutes)*

SCHEDULE FOR <u>FOUR</u> WEEKLY SESSIONS

Week 1   Date: _____

    Prayer Service: "Holy People—Sacred Places"   p. 11
    Lecture 1   p. 36
    Discussion Questions 1–6   p. 94
    Lecture 2   p. 43
    Closing (or *Prayer Service:* "Journeying Through Desert Trials"   p. 14)
    Personal Study—Complete Questions 7–12   p. 98

Week 2   Date: _____

    Prayer Service: "Through the Water to New Life"   p. 17
    Lecture 3   p. 48
    Discussion Questions 7–12   p. 98
    Lecture 4   p. 54
    Closing (or *Prayer Service:* "The Message From the Mountains"   p. 20)
    Personal Study—Complete Questions 13–18   p. 102

Week 3   Date: _____

    Prayer Service: "The Word Became Flesh and Dwelt Among Us"   p. 23
    Lecture 5   p. 61
    Discussion Questions 13–18   p. 102
    Lecture 6   p. 67
    Closing (or *Prayer Service:* "Release From Bondage"   p. 26)
    Personal Study—Complete Questions 19–24   p. 106

Week 4   Date: _____

    Prayer Service: "Pray for the Peace of Jerusalem"   p. 29
    Lecture 7   p. 76
    Discussion Questions 19–24   p. 106
    Lecture 8   p. 86
    Closing (or *Prayer Service:* "Inflame Our Hearts for Your Mission"   p. 32)

SCHEDULE FOR EIGHT WEEKLY SESSIONS

Week 1   Date: _____

Prayer Service: "Holy People—Sacred Places"   p. 11
Lecture 1   p. 36
Discussion Questions 1–3   p. 94
Closing
Personal Study—Complete Questions 4–6   p. 96

Week 2   Date: _____

Prayer Service: "Journeying Through Desert Trials"   p. 14
Lecture 2   p. 43
Discussion Questions 4–6   p. 96
Closing
Personal Study—Complete Questions 7–9   p. 98

Week 3   Date: _____

Prayer Service: "Through the Water to New Life"   p. 17
Lecture 3   p. 48
Discussion Questions 7–9   p. 98
Closing
Personal Study—Complete Questions 10–12   p. 100

Week 4   Date: _____

Prayer Service: "The Message From the Mountains"   p. 20
Lecture 4   p. 54
Discussion Questions 10–12   p. 100
Closing
Personal Study—Complete Questions 13–15   p. 102

Week 5   Date: _____

Prayer Service: "The Word Became Flesh and Dwelt Among Us" p. 23
Lecture 5   p. 61
Discussion Questions 13–15   p. 102
Closing

Personal Study—Complete Questions 16–18   p. 104

Week 6   Date: _____

Prayer Service: "Release From Bondage"   p. 26
Lecture 6   p. 67
Discussion Questions 16–18   p. 104
Closing

Personal Study—Complete Questions 19–21   p. 106

Week 7   Date: _____

Prayer Service: "Pray for the Peace of Jerusalem"   p. 29
Lecture 7   p. 76
Discussion Questions 19–21   p. 106
Closing

Personal Study—Complete Questions 22–24   p. 108

Week 8   Date: _____

Prayer Service: "Inflame Our Hearts for Your Mission"   p. 32
Lecture 8   p. 86
Discussion Questions 22–24   p. 108
Closing

Coordinator Responsibilities

1. Become totally familiar with the program as explained in this Leader's Guide.
2. Work with the pastor and parish leadership to:
   a. Plan and publicize the program.
   b. Choose and prepare small-group facilitators.
   c. Issue personal invitations to participate.
3. Follow the timeline provided in this Leader's Guide.
4. Order the materials.
5. Reserve the facilities and secure necessary equipment.
6. Conduct the weekly session, guiding the facilitators and participants through each stage of the program.
7. See that the sessions begin and end on schedule.
8. Delegate responsibilities to others; bring out the gifts that others have to share.
9. Plan a closing celebration.
10. Make a personal commitment to daily prayer and to the study of Scripture.

Support Team

A Support Team may be formed to help with the details of the program. Special needs may be:

SECRETARY / TREASURER

a. Collect registration fees and pay bills.
b. Prepare attendance records for each small group.
c. Prepare name tags; distribute and collect them each week.

PHYSICAL SET UP

a. Open doors; lock doors at end of session.
b. Check lecture room for: neatness, correct number of chairs, temperature, restroom supplies, etc.
c. Check group discussion areas for number of chairs.
d. Provide a speaker's stand with attached microphone.
e. Prepare set up for prayer services, choose readers.
f. Set up video tape player, monitor, and sound system.
g. Return rooms to order and put away supplies at end of session.

REFRESHMENTS

Organize refreshments for each session and for the closing celebration.

MUSIC MINISTRY

Choose suitable music and songbooks for prayer services. Recruit musicians and lead the singing.

TIMEKEEPER

Keep meetings running on schedule by reminding leaders of the time and giving a signal five minutes before the end of the small-group sharing.

CHILD CARE

Providing child care offers the opportunity for parents of small children to participate and increases attendance significantly. Children's Bible study, Bible stories, coloring, and crafts could be offered as a ministry to children.

Small-Group Facilitators

A facilitator is required for each group of eight to twelve. Facilitators should be well prepared for their role and familiar with this program. Participation in the Leadership Training sessions of Little Rock Scripture Study is ideal, though not required for this program.

Qualities to look for in a group facilitator:

- Ability to listen well and guide a group in an honest discussion;
- Capability to deal with a wide range of people and opinions and to keep a group focused and respectful of all;
- Familiarity with the Bible and previous experience in discussion groups;
- Has the time to devote to preparation and to be present each week;
- Exhibits a desire to deepen faith and serve others.

Techniques for the Small-Group Facilitator

SKILLS TO CULTIVATE

Set a climate of openness and love

Accept persons for who they are and where they are. Help the group members accept one another. Be sensitive to the feelings, moods, and needs of each person.

Be a good listener

Be attentive. Use eye contact, facial expression, and body posture. Don't interrupt. Be attuned to what is being said verbally and non-verbally.

Be supportive

Respect each person's ideas and feelings, especially the timid and those who have difficulty expressing themselves. Draw out the best each has to give. Praise insights and faith experiences shared. Be sensitive to those uncomfortable with personal faith sharing.

Be affirming

The group may have people from all walks of life—housewives, teachers, mechanics, doctors, plumbers, office workers, factory workers, retirees—with varying attitudes, values and knowledge.

Be encouraging

Some will have some knowledge of the Bible and experience at faith sharing; others very little. Encourage each in their efforts to be open to God's Word and one another.

Be a skillful questioner

A question can enlarge the group's vision of a topic or redirect the discussion if it wanders off the track.

Be responsive to the Holy Spirit working in the group

You are not the expert, but rather a fellow learner on the same faith journey seeking comfort, confidence, and challenge in God's Word.

Be familiar with destructive behavior

The dominator, rambler, or opinionated person can hinder the group's progress. Draw the focus back to the group by encouraging others to share.

POINTS TO KEEP IN MIND

- *You* set the tone for the group.
- Be prepared for the weekly sessions.
- Be attuned to the level of interest, ability, and knowledge of each member.

- Keep the discussion moving and focused on the lesson.
- Don't go around the group in a sequential order.
- Make good use of the allotted time.
- Don't be afraid of silence. It gives time to absorb what has been heard and helps formulate responses and sharing.
- Show you care by remembering the members' names, what you have learned about them, and some of the responses they have made.
- Keep in touch with those absent and encourage them in their efforts to participate.
- Keep your sense of humor. Christianity is a joyful experience.
- Trust in the Lord, the power of prayer, and the goodness of people.

Facilities and Equipment

Lands of the Bible requires a lecture area where all the participants may be comfortably seated. It also requires separate meeting spaces for each group of eight to twelve.

For the small-group discussion, arrange chairs in circles so that everyone can see one another. Use separate rooms or space the groups to limit distractions.

For the video lectures, a sufficiently large television or monitor and a video-cassette player is required. The chairs should be arranged so that all can see the screen without obstruction and glare. For groups of more than fifty, consider using multiple monitors with connecting cables from one player.

A place should be reserved in the front of the room for the Bible to be enthroned. This will be a place of focus during the prayer service and will remain throughout the session as a reverent reminder of the centrality of the Scriptures.

This arrangement can be easily adapted for groups meeting in homes. Assure that all members can see one another easily during the discussion and can see the TV screen for the lectures. Enthrone the Bible in a prominent place.

Preparations

REGISTRATION FEE

In setting the fee consider the amount of funds budgeted by the parish, the cost of the Participant's Books and the Leader's Guides, and other expenses.

PUBLICITY

Spur interest in the program with creative publicity. This may consist of church announcements, encouragement from the pastor, bulletin inserts, posters, and other creative means.

RECRUITMENT

Personal invitations are the most effective. Telephone calls, an invitation at the Sunday Eucharist, sign-up on Sundays, and personal letters or postcards are all effective. Urge those who have never participated in a Scripture study because of unfamiliarity with the Bible to join this program.

MATERIALS

Order a Participant's Book for each leader and participant, a Leader's Guide for each leader, and a set of the eight taped lectures at least four weeks in advance.

Order sufficient books for every possible participant as unused books may be returned within one month of the order date.

PRAYER SERVICES

The preparations for these prayer services are simple but necessary so that a reflective tone can be set at the beginning of the session. The following suggestions will help to prepare for the service each week:

- Choose readers for the Scripture passages well in advance so that they will have time to practice. Choose those who are confident enough to proclaim the Word.

- The environment, music, and prayer symbols should reflect reverence for the Word and attention to the theme of each week's service. Symbols appropriate for the theme of each prayer service may be added each week. The seventh prayer service requires that participants face the East, and the eighth service requires that a candle be lit.
- Enthrone the Bible in a prominent place, with one or two candles lit during the prayer service. Readers may use this Bible for the readings.
- To help participants be comfortable with the particulars of each week's service, go through the order of the service before beginning, pointing out the places where they are to respond.
- After giving the welcome and instructions for the prayer service, begin with a few moments of quiet to set a reflective tone. Ask the participants to set aside the burdens of the day and realize that God is in their midst; then proceed with the service.
- Begin the prayer service with a song. Music appropriate to the theme of each service are listed here.

"Holy People—Sacred Places"

"Canticle of the Sun"
"Companions on the Journey"
"Glory and Praise to Our God"
"God Beyond All Names"
"Holy Ground"
"How Great Thou Art"
"Let All Things Now Living"
"May We Praise You"

"Journeying Through Desert Trials"

"Be Not Afraid"
"For You Are My God"
"The Glory of These Forty Days"
"Lead Me, Guide Me"
"Shelter Me, O God"
"We Walk by Faith"
"We Will Drink the Cup"
"You Are Near"

"Through the Water to New Life"

"Come to the Water"
"Healing River"
"I Want to Walk As a Child of the Light"
"Shall We Gather at the River"
"Song over the Waters"
"Swing Low Sweet Chariot"
"Two Fishermen"
"Water of Life"
"You Have Put on Christ"

"The Message from the Mountains"

"Christ upon the Mountain Peak"
"On Eagle's Wings"
"Sing a New Song"
"Sing to the Mountains"
"Though the Mountains May Fall"

"The Word Became Flesh and Dwelt Among Us"

"Angels We Have Heard on High"
"The First Noël"
"Gloria"
"Go Tell It on the Mountain"
"He Came Down"
"Lo, How a Rose E'er Blooming"
"Love Divine, All Loves Excelling"
"O Little Town of Bethlehem"
"People, Look East"
"Silent Night"
"What Child Is This"

"Release from Bondage"

"Amazing Grace"
"Blest Be the Lord"
"Let There Be Peace on Earth"
"Prayer of Peace"
"Prayer of St. Francis"
"There's a Wideness in God's Mercy"
"Thy Kingdom Come"
"When Jesus Came Preaching the Kingdom of God"
"You Are Mine"

"Pray for the Peace of Jerusalem"

"City of God"
"The Holy City"
"How Great Thou Art"
"If I Forget You"
"Jerusalem My Destiny"
"Praise to the Lord, the Almighty"

"Inflame Our Hearts for Your Mission"

"Christ Be Our Light"
"The Church's One Foundation"
"Come Holy Ghost"
"Come Down, O Love Divine"
"Companions on the Journey"
"Gather Us In"
"God Has Chosen Me"
"God's Blessing Sends Us Forth"
"Go Make of All Disciples"
"In Christ There Is No East or West"
"I Received the Living God"
"I Will Be with You"
"Lift High the Cross"
"Lord of All Nations, Grant Me Grace"
"Rejoice the Lord Is King"
"We Are Many Parts"
"We Walk by Faith"

REFRESHMENTS/CLOSING CELEBRATION

Simple refreshments may be provided each week. These may be taken to the small-group discussion, served at a break, or at the end of the session.

It is a good idea to plan a closing celebration. Some options would be a potluck preceding the final session or a social at the conclusion of the program. The celebration might also include time for participants to share with the entire group what the course has meant to them and to plan for future programs.

Timeline for Preparation

EIGHT WEEKS BEFORE THE PROGRAM BEGINS

- Discuss the program with the pastor and parish leadership. Set the dates and registration fee.
- Reserve facilities and video equipment.
- Plan publicity and recruitment.

SIX WEEKS BEFORE THE PROGRAM BEGINS

- Recruit facilitators (one for each group of eight to twelve).
- Recruit a support team to help with the details of the program.
- Publicize and personally invite participants.

FOUR WEEKS BEFORE THE PROGRAM BEGINS

- Continue publicity and invitations and sign up participants.
- Order the taped lectures, a Leader's Guide for each facilitator, and a Participant's Book for every possible participant.
- Pray with the facilitators and support team for the success of the program.

TWO WEEKS BEFORE THE PROGRAM BEGINS

- Assign the small groups.
- Prepare name tags. This designates groups and helps participants learn the names of one another. Indicate on the name tags (with a number, color, Scripture verse, etc.) the small group of each person.
- Meet with the facilitators and support team to make final arrangements and assignments and to pray together.

Directions for the First Session

WELCOME/INTRODUCTION

Greet participants as they arrive.

Give each a name tag, group assignment, and copy of the Participant's Book.

Welcome participants as the session begins and give a brief introduction to the program and the process of each weekly session. Encourage faithful attendance and commitment to the small group.

PRAYER SERVICE

Bible is enthroned; that is, set open on a stand or placed in the center of a table reverently prepared. Candles should be lit.

Other symbols, appropriate to the theme or season may be added.

Leader of prayer should indicate which side of the room will be "left" and which will be "right" for the response at some of the prayer services.

Begin with a few moments of quiet to set a reflective tone.

LECTURES

Refer participants to the outlines for each lecture in their Participant's Book. Encourage them to add their own notes if they wish. Play the video lecture.

SMALL-GROUP DISCUSSION

Direct participants to their assigned groups to discuss the questions indicated on the schedule.

You may also ask: "What were the main insights you received from the lecture you just watched?"

Facilitators should not feel obliged to discuss every question. Choose those that seem most helpful and complete others if time allows.

Call groups back after the allotted time even though groups may not have finished the discussion. It is important to remain on time.

CONCLUSION

Encourage reading and study during the week. Assign "Questions for Study and Discussion." Session may conclude with a brief prayer or blessing.

Use and Care of Video Tapes

- Keep the tape away from high temperatures, excessive dust, and moisture.
- Keep the tape away from strong magnetic fields, such as TV sets or speakers.
- Do not leave the cassette exposed directly to the sun.
- Do not attempt to open the cassette. Do not touch the tape.
- To prevent accidental damage to the tape and recorder caused by moisture from condensation, be sure that the videotape is kept at room temperature for at least one hour before being used. Use of a cold tape in a warm recorder could result in the formation of moisture on the tape, which might damage the tape or recorder.
- Avoid repeated insertion and removal of the tape without operating the machine. If the machine fails to function as desired when the Play, Rewind, or Fast Forward button is pressed, check that the tape is not at either end of its travel.
- Always store the tape in the cassette case when it is to be carried or mailed, or when it is not to be used for a long time.
- Do not drop the tape. Avoid violent vibrations or shock.
- Do not repeat loading and unloading a tape without playing the tape. This may cause tape slack and result in damage to the tape.
- Unlike an audio tape, the videotape may be used on only one side.

Answer Guide

This Answer Guide contains some suggested responses for the "Questions for Study and Discussion." It gives factual answers to some questions and offers direction and guidance for others. Its use is restricted to the *facilitators only.*

Facilitators are encouraged to prepare their own lesson for the week before referring to the Answer Guide. After completing the lesson, facilitators may look over the Answer Guide to make sure they have a good understanding of each question so that they can guide the group discussion more effectively.

The Answer Guide should not be displayed or mentioned during the small-group discussion. If group members know there is an Answer Guide, many will be tempted to wait for the "right answer" instead of recognizing and developing their own ability to learn from Scripture.

1. a. God has entered into relationship with our biblical ancestors in historical time and in particular places. The more we can understand these places, the more we can understand the context and meaning of the saving events of the Bible. In studying the biblical places, we are able to compare them to the "places" of our own lives, and understand better how God enters into relationship with us in the context of particular people, times, and places.

   b. Personal responses will vary. Responses may include homes of childhood and adulthood, churches, places that hold memories of challenges, growth, loving commitment, sickness, death, and life transitions.

2. a. A pilgrimage is a journey to a sacred place in search of God. It is a separation from ordinary life in order to experience life in a new way and acquire new insights and perceptions for daily living.

   b. Pilgrimage is an outward journey of traveling to a new place and an inward journey in which we experience God in a new way. Through imagination, prayer, and liturgy, we experience the saving events associated with the sacred place and thus experience its effects in our own lives.

   c. Personal responses will vary.

3. a. Throughout his life Jesus followed the Jewish tradition by going on pilgrimage to Jerusalem for the feasts. The Gospel of John indicates that Jesus went up to Jerusalem frequently throughout his public life. The pilgrimages of Jesus help us realize that Jesus was a traditional Jew, that traveling to the sacred places of his tradition was important, and that pilgrimage was an important part of his own internal, spiritual growth.

   b. Jesus observed the pilgrim feasts of Passover, Pentecost, and Tabernacles.

4. a. Personal responses will vary. Experiences may include immigration, seeking refuge, moving to a new home, etc. Events and descriptions of feelings will vary.

   b. Abraham and Sarah had to leave all that was comfortable and secure for them. They had no certainty about their destination. They traveled through risky, unknown country, and they knew they had to depend on God's guidance. Responses will vary when describing personal experiences teaching faith and trust.

5. The desert is associated with trial and testing. As Jesus was preparing for his public ministry, he went to the desert to be tested by God and to experience the hardship that would prepare him to do God's will. Jesus followed in the ways of his Hebrew ancestors who went to the desert to be tried and tested as they entered into covenant with God. In the solitude of the desert Jesus reflected on God's will and gained a deeper understanding of his mission.

6. a. Personal responses will vary. Experiences of the desert may include times of confusion about life choices, times of grief, times of solitary prayer and reflection, tests of faith, experiences of spiritual dryness and barrenness, and times of painful transition.

   b. Individuals will vary both in their own experiences of trial and in their comparisons with the biblical experiences.

7. a. The great flood, the embalming of Jacob, Moses on Mount Sinai, Israel in the desert, Elijah traveling to Mount Sinai, Jesus in the wilderness, and resurrection appearances of Jesus.

   b. The forty days and nights of the great flood in preparation for a renewed creation; the forty days of embalming and burying

Jacob as a transition between the age of the patriarchs and the exodus; the forty days and nights at Mount Sinai in preparation for receiving the covenant; the forty years of Israel in the desert as a transition from bondage to freedom in the land; the forty days and nights of Elijah as preparation to encounter God at Mount Sinai; the forty days and nights of Jesus as he fasted in the desert as a transition between his private life and his ministry; and the forty days of Jesus' resurrection appearances as the transition from his life on earth to his ascension into heaven.

8. a. Descriptions will vary. Responses may describe a flood, a storm, swimming or boating in danger, near drowning, etc.

   b. Responses may include descriptions of beaches, watching soothing waves, lakes, boating, swimming, ice water on a hot day, water to quench the thirst, etc.

9. a. The great flood, Israel crossing the Red Sea, Israel crossing the Jordan River, Jacob crossing the Jabbok River, Elijah and Elisha crossing the Jordan River, the baptism of Jesus, and Christian baptism.

   b. This crossing the waters symbolizes the many ways in which we cross over from one stage of life to another. Between stages there is often an obstacle or a boundary that must be crossed before we can move on. There is a dying to one stage of life and rising to a renewed life.

10. a. Responses might include baptism, sprinkling rituals, Easter water, washing of feet, baptismal renewal, etc.

    b. Water represents dying and rising in Christ, dying to our old life and rising to new life, cleansing from sin, humble service, and reminders of baptism.

11. a. A map showing the division of Canaan into the twelve tribes would show most of the places mentioned: Giliad, Dan, Naphtali, Ephraim, Manasseh, Judah, the Mediterranean Sea, the Negeb, the Jordan River, Jericho.

    b. Responses will vary.

12. a. The number forty is used in reference to the journey of both Moses and Elijah. Moses spent forty days and nights on the

mountain; Elijah spent forty days and nights traveling to the mountain. Through Moses, God revealed the covenant to Israel on the mountain. Elijah was to reestablish the covenant with Israel after his journey to Sinai. God's presence was revealed to Moses with signs of wind, storm, earthquake and fire. Elijah realized that those signs were not God's presence but that God's presence was a more subtle manifestation like a whispering wind.

    b. Responses will vary. The more powerful manifestations of God suggest that God is uncontrolled, almighty, powerful, unpredictable, startling, and unable to be contained. The whispering sound seems to suggest that God's presence is personal, interior, spiritual, and difficult to perceive.

13. Personal responses will vary.

14. a. In the Gospel of Luke, Mary is the mother of Jesus and the model of discipleship. Her maternity and her virginity are emphasized to express both the humanity and the divinity of Jesus. Her receptivity and obedience to God's word is expressed in her response to the divine message: "Let it be done to me according to your word." She is called "mother of my Lord" by Elizabeth. Her double role as mother of the Lord and model disciple are emphasized by Elizabeth's words: "Blessed are you among women, and blessed is the fruit of your womb," and "Blessed is she who believed that there would be a fulfillment of what was spoken to her by the Lord."

    b. Mary symbolizes the Church in that she brings Christ to birth in the world and represents all disciples as they respond in obedience to God's Word. Thus, people around the world represent her as one like themselves. She represents their own role as disciples of Jesus.

15. a. Responses will vary. The visit of Mary and Elizabeth demonstrates that friends often surpass distance and obstacles to be together in times of need, that friends encourage faith and trust in one another, that friends express and confirm for each other the interior voices and movements of God.

    b. Responses will vary. A young person can teach an older person about God's surprising ways and how to respond to God with enthusiasm and spontaneity. An old person can teach a younger person about the importance of acceptance and faithfulness in relationship to God and how to learn from the experiences, failures, and challenges of life.

16. a. Bethlehem was the birthplace of King David and thus was associated through the prophets with the birthplace of the Messiah.

   b. In a small town, in a simple place, among poor and lowly people, the Word was made flesh and dwelt among us. Bethlehem teaches us that God works in humble places, with humble people, to accomplish great things.

17. a. Because the paralytic was unable to get to Jesus himself, four friends opened the roof and lowered him down with ropes.

   b. Some people are unable to come to Jesus themselves because of their fears or uncertainties, because they don't know how, or because they have never received the invitation or encouragement to come.

   c. This scene demonstrates that friendship in Christ is important because we need other people to bring us to Christ. Friends can support us, give us new insights, challenge us, and guide us along life's way.

18. a. The second account of the loaves and fish takes place in Gentile territory. It occurs during the part of Mark's Gospel in which Jesus is traveling in Tyre, Sidon, and the district of the Decapolis—all areas filled with non-Jewish people.

   b. In the first account there are five loaves and twelve baskets of fragments; in the second account there are seven loaves with seven baskets of fragments.

   c. The number twelve often represents the people of Israel, designated as twelve tribes or Jacob's twelve sons. The number seven symbolizes an infinite or universal amount. The seven loaves and baskets represents the universal extent of the Christian mission and the endless number of people who are called to be nourished by Christ.

19. a. Capernaum was the home base for Jesus and his disciples. Jesus stayed often at the house of Peter and his family. Jesus often

taught in the synagogue there. The close relationship that Jesus experienced with his disciples in Capernaum was necessary for them to accept his difficult teaching while many others turned away.

    b. Personal responses may include ways that we have experienced Jesus as spiritual nourishment, as satisfaction for the hungers of our souls, as Eucharistic Communion, as food for a starving world.

    c. After this sermon of Jesus, many of his disciples turned away and no longer followed him. Peter's response teaches us that Jesus is the only one who speaks the words of eternal life. Peter teaches us to trust the words of Jesus and to put our confidence in him.

20. a. Jesus was angry because the Temple of God's presence was being abused and desecrated.

    b. Jesus proclaimed his risen life as the new temple because it would be the certain place to seek God. When the old Temple would be in ruins, the temple of his body, the Church, would manifest a renewed presence of God among humanity.

    c. 1 Peter 2:4-6 proclaims that we are the living stones, chosen by God, to be built into a spiritual temple, offering spiritual sacrifices through our lives in Christ. Ephesians 2:19-22 proclaims that we are all being built into God's temple with the apostles and prophets as the foundation and Jesus Christ as the capstone.

21. Personal responses will vary. Jesus spent his last week visiting his friends in Bethany, teaching, proclaiming justice, praying in the garden, seeking to accept his impending death, and bearing his suffering with confident courage.

22. a. Responses will vary. The prayer of Jesus teaches us the importance of solitude with God, the importance of prayerful support from friends, the appropriateness of emotion in prayer, and the necessity of asking God for acceptance.

    b. Jesus needed personal support from his closest friends in his hour of need.

    c. Personal responses.

23. a. Responses may include surprised, confused, defensive, insecure, perplexed, disappointed, etc.
    b. Personal experiences will differ. Participants may describe times in which their first-impressions or prejudices prevented them from truly knowing another person.
    c. Personal responses will vary.
24. a. Examples will vary. Mission statements may include important goals, priorities, and motivations.
    b. Participants should be encouraged to compare their understanding of Jesus' mission to their own goals, priorities, and motivations.
    c. Personal responses will vary. Participants should be encouraged to summarize the lessons of this series by speaking about their own lives as pilgrimage.

NOTES